WHO WALKS AMONG THE TREES WITH CHARITY

WHO WALKS AMONG THE TREES
WITH CHARITY

CHRISTINE SWANBERG

Christine Swanberg (signature)

WIND PUBLICATIONS

International Standard Book Number 1893239357
Library of Congress Control Number 2005920297

First edition

Other books and chapbooks by Christine Swanberg

Tonight on This Late Road. Erie Street Press, Oak Park, IL. 1984. Henry Kranz, Publisher.
Invisible String. Erie Street Press. Oak Park, IL. 1990. Henry Kranz, Publisher.
Bread Upon the Waters. University of Wisconsin: Whitewater, Windfall Prophets Press, Whitewater, WI. 1990. Ron Ellis, Publisher.
Slow Miracle. Lakeshore Publishing, Deerfield, IL. 1992. Carol Spelius, Publisher.
The Tenderness of Memory. Plainview Press. Austin, TX. 1995. Susan Bright, Publisher.
The Red Lacquer Room. Chiron Press. St. John, KS. 2001. Michael Hathaway, Publisher.

Front and rear cover photographs by Jeff Swanberg.

The author thanks the editors of the following publications where these poems first appeared or were anthologized:

Amelia: "Oppenheimer After Forty Years"
American Massage Journal: "Masseuse"
Bolinas Poems Au Natural: "Marin Muse"
Butterfly Chronicles: "Grocery," "Tiger Wing," "Marin Muse," "Meandering"
Chiron: "Paris on $5 a Day," "My Private James," "What a Gardener Knows About Change"
Connections: "Let Indian Summer Come"
Dan River Anthology: "For Zachary Beach," "Key West"
Earth's Daughters: "The Man at the Pool"
English Journal: "Sonnet For Live Words"
Great Old Broads: "When Less is More"
Kansas Quarterly: "Tape"
Glass Cherry: "Fort Zachary Beach," "Key West"
Kansas Quarterly: "Tape"
Korone: "A Friend Asks," "Opportunity," "Mira Makes it To Samos"
Mid-America Poetry Review: "The Uses of Winter," "January Rain," "Swimming," "One Cold February Morning," "Amidst Prairie Grass"
Midwest Poetry Review: "Lighthouse"
Moon Journal: "Summer Solstice," "Embrace Uncertainty," "Nevertheless"
Nit And Wit: "Prairie Burner"
Out Of Line: "Epiphany," "The Tree Trimmers," "Sparrows Falling From the Sky"
Peninsula Pulse: "At Three Arch Cape," "Poem to my Retirement"
Peninsula Review: "Lines Written for Charlotte in Bronte Country"
Poets Ink: "The Empty Bowl," "Opportunity"
PoetsWest: "Again on the Road to Tillamook," "The Red Lacquer Room," "Piano Lessons," "Hope Chest," "At Three Arch Cape," "The Rings of Saturn," "Winter Spell"
Powhatan Review: "O° of Separation," "Whippoorwill," "Smile Poem Found at the Bank"
Prairie Winds: "Dream of Only a Porpoise," "Reconciled with Winter," "Forgive Me, Sisters," "To Love my Country"

Rock River Times: "How the Road Saved Us"
Rockford Review: "Food"
Sandstar: "Letter to John Lennon," "Remembering a Line from Stanley Kunitz"
Slant: "Genealogy"
Snowy Egret: "Dream Bandits"
Spoon River Quarterly: "At the Train Station," "Before Grooming the Horse in Winter"
Tambourine: "Wide Wisconsin Prairie," "The Red Lacquer Room," "Rings of Saturn," "Whippoorwill," "Poem to My Retirement"
Towers: "Mornings in Moscow," "A Remembrance for Panajachel"
Windfall: "The Christmas Tree Lot," "Because"
Wisconsin Review: "Meandering"
Sow's Ear: "Four Virtues Revisited"
Wind: "Point of Departure"

"Oppenheimer, After Forty Years" was nominated for a Pushcart prize.

"The Red Lacquer Room" was featured in a juried competition by the Chicago Poetry Center.

This book is dedicated to

Geno Rinaldi, my father,

1924-2004

Contents

THE GRACE OF THE GENTLE UNAMBITIOUS

AMONG THE TREES WITH CHARITY

Genealogy

Genealogy

Suppose just one root of the family tree
Went west instead of east
Or that just one renegade seed sprouted
From the canon of ancestors
And remained unnamed. Then Great-
Grandfather Sinclair might have been Ojibwa.
Just one root might trace primordially
To a medicine man named Sees-with-Three-Eyes.
His wife, whose blood tom toms
Through your veins, might have woven baskets
In a Moon Lodge with many of your cousins,
Whose names might be Eagle-Talon
Or Two-Antelopes-Leaping.
If just one branch of the family tree
Were grafted, the name of its hybrid offshoot
Not written in the lexicon of heritage, then
Great-Great Nana Sarah might really have been
A gypsy whose line disappeared under Hitler.
Her black Bohemian mane enchanting men.
Her gift for song unmatched. Her dexterity
A legend not told. Isn't it likely that the family tree
Has been exposed to genetic detours here and there?
A few places where the leaves don't match?
A patch where the bark suddenly whorls?
Think of the possibilities: Mongolian peasant,
Spanish Jew, Teutonic slave, Madagascan midwife.
Keep going back and you might find
A black bear hibernating, a black bat hanging,
A two-toed sloth, buzzard, ruby-throated hummingbird,
A bullhead bottom feeder, a pterodactyl,
A butterfly painted with a question mark,
A small green snake, a whorled blue barnacle,
Maybe something extinct and never named,
A living spark from the great cosmic tumble,
A dent in the DNA.

Prairie Burner

This Sheyela of the white man
is a good horse: small and red
with yellow mane, worth seven beaded
pouches, three moons and a deerskin.
My legs fit around her body
like moccasins. Heels touch the curve
of her belly. One heel—she moves gentle.
Two—we thunder cornstalks
soon before the snow. Our breath
blends in the wind above her mane.

Today we go to burn the prairie.
This is our kindness to the buffalo:
Huge bodies but teeth like corn kernels,
too small to mulch the woody underbrush.
The buffalo cannot eat trees, or swim,
or build himself a home. He wanders
the prairie like my people.

By the river Sheyela's ears turn:
the pheasant flies: the mouse slides
under leaf: the red-tail circles.
I rub the flint together
in the driest underbrush. Sheyela waits.
I have taught her our purpose
and not to fear the small suns
that will fill the air with sweet
prairie wood smoke. All night upon Sheyela

I will watch the fire spread: flames
of spirits dancing as the sun turns river red.
The prairie becomes the burning knees
of the Wind Spirit, pushed to the river's arm.

After four moons of snow, the buffalo
will graze here and grow strong
for I am Prairie Burner, keeper of the buffalo.

Swimming

Whenever I slide into the cold water,
dive under to get used to it,
gliding like a dolphin for a moment
beneath the water's silky surface,
I am grateful that no one made me fear
this chilly pleasure. I remember watching
Esther Williams with my mother.
I'm four and unafraid under the movie's
dark canopy, where my mother and I eat
homemade popcorn from a waxy paper bag,
munching languorously as manatees.
The sticky salt on my fingers and the faint smell
of algae from the theater's spores,
Esther Williams opening like a water lily,
and I was hooked on swimming,
hair slicked back like an otter's,
the porous magic of weightlessness,
the Yoga-like asana of graceful breaststroke,
feet pointed and agile as a ballerina's.
Some of us are born for the plunge.
Some of us get only to the edge, dangle feet
in icy water, pass a tadpole boldness on
to someone bound to use it.

The Christmas Tree Lot

Blue spruces, big as phantoms
in a little girl's dream, stacked
frozen, like cards from the Queen of Hearts,
and those Norway pines—an evergreen
profusion where I learned
the love of men, bristled and aromatic,
in their plaid mufflers and orange
coats. The tree keeper, snow wedged
in his soles, gave my uncle
coffee in the sanctuary hut. Sitting
at the old table in my blue
snow suit, I listened
to the laughter of business partners.
I was perfectly happy, nothing
demanded, sweetly ignored, perhaps
some small joy, like making
a snow angel in the parking lot.

Hope Chest

The wide jaw of Aunt Lillian's old cedar chest opens—
what is left of her life now
that she shuffles behind her walker,
steps smaller than a foot-bound concubine's,
mumbling in the oven-warm room
at a place where the food is soft
and plentiful.
          What is left: bright towel sets, never used—
chartreuse, burnt orange, fuchsia, lilac, and aqua.
These must have been bought in the wild Sixties,
a time she missed altogether
except for this garish stash of terry cloth. Retro—
the college kids call it.
          Foraging deeper
into that musty bin, eyes stinging,
I find the mother lode of vintage tablecloths—
a baker's dozen of wild retros: enormous grapes,
golden pears, sienna apples, cerulean lattice;
Frida Kahlo flowers exploding on white cotton;
wheat shafts sewn on coarse beige linen;
an embarrassment of pert napkins;
hand-painted lobelia on shiny scotch plaid;
two Scandinavian-fringed blue and red broadcloths;
ecru damask ringed in teal paisley.
What was she thinking?
          Retro: She's 22, dreams
of picnics on the river: ham sandwiches and apples,
a sweetheart not unlike Dean Martin;
a dining room of her own where Thanksgiving is served;
learning to drive. None of this happened.
She worked for 50 years, rose
to Head Cook at Saint Joseph's Hospital,
made ribbon jello for Thanksgiving

at my childhood table; ate between shifts.
Now someone does the same for her.
Now it's her turn to say the food is lousy.

I have washed, starched, and ironed the tablecloths,
placed one on the dining room maple,
another over the soda parlor table on the porch,
given two to friends who definitely dig Retro.
Tomorrow my husband and I will drive
a vintage ice-blue bathtub Porsche to Harrington Beach,
on Lake Michigan's lapping shores, the inland sea.
The wind will catch the corners
of the lovely vintage tablecloth
before we spread our picnic: brown crackers,
Wisconsin smoked cheddar,
apples from the farmers' market,
Merlot in long-stemmed glasses.
                    The gulls
will be mad with envy. Swallows will swoop
from their honeycomb nests on high sandy shelves.
The bloody-nose trillium may snub us.
If we're politically correct, we'll call it an Indian Moccasin—
not unlike the one Pocahontas may have worn
the day she met the captain she would marry,
before her large life galloped ahead.

Tape

Just in case someone wants to steal
the $5 bill in the big, pink

envelope, Aunt Libby tapes the sides.
Aunt Lurette did this too

but I blamed it on The Depression.
The first time a bandaged integument

arrived—my ninth birthday—I thought
it looked like appendix scars. Matching.

Once, when a holiday delayed the mail,
Lurette went into a weeklong dither.

Poor darling, she finally crossed her i's
instead of her t's. Oh, I know

old age isn't funny, the aunts are dear,
and I'm grateful to be thought of innocently

as a niece—and at least Aunt Libby's not
double-taping yet, garbling

those poor, little pockets with crossed
wires, forgetting to sign her name,

or even taping the bill inside the card
(which always made me think of mud flaps.)

But Libby's b's have lost vitality;
she's almost Aunt Lilly now, folding

the bill inside the Hallmark, taping
its sides as if that weren't a dead give-away.

Surely there's a word for morbid fear of checks.
A flimsy word that holds but cannot cure.

Piano Lessons

Whenever I hear Rhapsody in Blue—
its high notes taking off like yellow cabbage moths,
its twisted and turbulent augmentations—
I feel the kind, thin, succulent-veined hand
of Mrs. Christiansen, my piano teacher.
It lands and brushes my right wrist,
settling like a brown, spotted elfin moth.
She's affirming my meager meanderings
on the cherry wood piano that smells of Lemon Pledge.
She's with me all the way through
Now-I-start-with-lesson-one.
Making-music-is-such-fun;
Blue Nocturne (which turned me on in fifth grade
bent as I was already toward the erotic.)
She's snapping her sallow, freckled fingers
to that Dog Gone Boogie
(which I probably butchered);
nodding tight-lipped and wide-eyed
as my short but nimble fingers
flayed out The Flight of the Bumble Bee.
Her right hand is drawn up to her neck
during Autumn Leaves
(which I probably pruned the life out of).
Any Rimsky-Korsakov or Tchaikovsky sent her
into glazed-over Buddhahood. Dear Mrs. Christiansen,
who recognized another hopeless romantic
when she saw one, who had the good sense
to know I'd never make it to Virtuoso
and didn't press the issue. Because of this,
I have loved the piano ever since,
however unmagnificent the solos to my cat may be.
In those three years before both our bodies blistered
out of control—hers with cancer

that turned her skin to beeswax
and made her apartment give off an odor
like ripe donuts; mine ajar with hormones
and pheromones so potent I lost my taste
for music and went fortissimo for boys—
we enjoyed each other's company,
bedazzled and drawn toward a startling luminescence.

If Love Were

Forgive me, Sisters

For I love men—
lollipop men, sweet enough to lick,
banana men, ripe and peeled,
smooth shaven men with long hair,
sweaty men in dusty boots,
daring men in fast blue cars,
rich, brooding Rochester men,
renegade, reckless Heathcliff men,
Ojibwa men hooping and dancing,
brothers, daddies, and single men,
rocking and singing black preacher men,
doctors with kind gray eyes and bow ties,
high Peter Fonda motorcycle men,
sad, guitar strumming Bob Dylan men,
smiling old men holding doors,
handy men fixing engines and toasters,
industrious men building stairs,
men who chip in around the house,
massaging men who give foot rubs,
slow-to-anger men, who love women,
fun loving men in open Hawaiian shirts,
swimming men, driving men, men on tractors,
men with sunburned hands and twinkling eyes,
funny men who laugh at women's jokes,
men with loud, infectious laughs,
men who do things women don't want to do,
men who paint garages and wax cars,
men who like mutts and bad cats,
men who marry and don't stray,
men who don't betray,
men who carry, lift, push, and haul,
men who marry women they love,
men who love women more than they love men.

0° of Separation

Living in your hometown
the mailman turns out to be
your first lover. Thirty years
and now he's paunchy
like his father, just the way
you remember him at dinner,
his big Irish Catholic family
eating potatoes with ketchup,
the dark dining room that smells
cruciferous, the bronze crucifix
hovering over Sylvia and Patty,
who were sure to be spinsters.
And you, even then wanting
to bolt, knowing already
in some starchy place: You
could never do this. Knowing
already that mama's boys
make the meanest lovers.
In your hometown, the mailman
makes his rounds. Today he
wears Bermudas and white sox.
This is the man you betrayed,
the young man whose lottery number
was up, who called you Tiger
in the stoned-out letters
you never kept, whose mother loathed
you with good reason. He earned
his stripes and so did you,
Tiger, Tiger, burning bright,
too young to be true.

Reconciled With Winter

I am one grown reconciled with winter
with its blizzard of losses. Snowflakes
shimmer on my lashes, melt,
trickle down my warm cheekbone.

The wind of errors blows
through bare birch branches
seared double white. Smoke
from our mouths—

before the glacial freeze
and its numbing confusion of ice.
No going back. Ever.
Today a foot of snow

forces us deeper inside separate
sanctuaries and Siberian drifts,
leave us stranded by the fires
of our separate hearths, burning

domestic and safe like layered riders
in Russian coaches pulled by dark horses
whose carved bells make a bleak harpsichord
this bittersweet winter twilight.

Venus smolders near the silver-ice moon.
Remember me as one who brought you
burgundy boots from Moscow,
the warmest suede vest from Kiev,

a beaded basket of black seeds,
the wildest of oats scattered
in a field of wheat. Never sown.
And though I know you gave the precious

cargo to someone else, discarded
it like the most beautiful and interesting
veined red maple leaves, almost kept,
I have grown reconciled with winter.

Remember me as one who rides
red horses in the snow, their bells
ring merry nonetheless. Remember me
as one who wakes to brilliance,

the winter sun severe, its sheaf of heat
slanting through the blue gauze curtains.

My Private James

You come to me in winter
from a field of wild, wild wheat
that is covered with ashes of snow.
Innocent. Open
as the wide, Wisconsin prairie
in the heart of the Kettle Morraine
where we lived on lakes
named Golden, Eagle, or Lorraine.
Freedom
was a feeling, not
something earned.
You were my private James.
James as in Morrison or Dean.
You were my private 1969,
the year I went to Russia,
hightailed to Woodstock
without you;
the year you quit school twice,
snapped me like an Indian bow
in your leaving like a hunter
out for fresh kill.
Now, thirty years apart from you,
I see I am the survivor,
and you a great loss
in my manuscript of losses.
You, with your sweet skin
of wind and wheat.
You with your Rich Boy cruelty.
Because I will not betray a finer man
to hunt you down
as I did time after time
in those innocent-wicked days
before I earned my freedom

before I learned that cruelty
was a pebble in my own fist all along,
you will never read this.
You will never
know I did not lose my great adventure.
I've been to places
called Lugano, Kaanapali, and
Chichicastenango. You will
never
know how much I wish the same for
you.

A Dream of Only a Porpoise

On my knees, gardening in the back yard
amongst familiar stones and dark soil,
blue hyacinths pushing up leafy mulch,
when a large, glossy bird casts a shadow
over the gray fence, circles closer,
rounds the Drake maple, jangles the wispy
river birch branches like Moroccan beads.

When I look up, the sky is a blinding
Genovese blue, the sun stings like chlorine,
and that's when I see it—a huge, flying porpoise
awkwardly landing, a thud on moist ground.
He stands the way a penguin does.
I stand too, for reasons only the dream knows,
confused and intoxicated in the spring air.

He wants to play, butts his sleek black chest,
rippling rubber against my shoulder.
We're doing some geriatric Watusi
in the garden which has grown insignificant.
The porpoise is clearly smiling and his eyes
are evolved beyond his specie. He could be
a dark angel or a powerful sexual desire.

Later, when night's velvet curtain pulls open
its dream proscenium, the story continues
though the porpoise who has no name is not there.
Just my dear husband and I, and I am saying,
"I'm in love with a porpoise." He says,
"Thank God. I thought there was someone else."
"No. There's no one else," I say. "Only a porpoise."

The Uses of Winter

Suppose that winter were a license
to be like trees and bears,
a simple barren time of sleep and fur,
snoring and cuddling,
the drawing of deep, cold water
from black root and river bottom,
the best long rest by fire, brightest
January sun through bare branches.

Suppose that winter were a drug,
splash of morphine on the rocks,
and the simplest chores, say
polishing silver spoons, suddenly
shows you the lost art of embossing:
a sheaf of wheat on a curved handle,
a thumbnail bear, MISSOURI: Do people
really live there? Do they love company?

Suppose the winter wind that scalps
the leafless Norway maple and makes
the weeping willow brush the river's icy
edge has nothing to do with you
hibernating in the blue comforter
awakened only by the lover you haven't named,
your invisible winter lover, dream
of climax unexpected and complete.

Suppose that winter were a white wolf
resurrected, a howl within your ribs
that longs for icy solitude, that place
where all the pleasant masks are hung
to dry beside red, wet parkas,
the cheery, nubby mittens, the closet
where the one ferocious muse
finally has her way with you.

Whippoorwill

If love were a whippoorwill, he would fly
to me in Indian Summer. We'd spiral

high against the golden autumn sky,
dive for last dreamy dusky-winged moths,

loop around the poplar tops over and over
until we'd had our fill. I'd accept

dark chimneys of sleep, the sacred soot
and smoke, cool dormancy we must keep

in order to endure. We'd take each day,
every harbored snowfall. Who knows why

some hearts open again like the dwarf red rose,
tender perennial, or why some cease for keeps.

Where does he vanish, the whippoorwill who
does not come again, his forlorn call?

Last night I dreamed he wrapped me
in his wings. We were quiet long and then

he sang his wild summer song. We sailed above
the scraggy trees, chased the sun that sets behind

the long, black chimneys. When the furious breeze
allowed, we arced between the moon and Venus.

We survived, didn't we—you and I—when clouds
like whippoorwills' wings wisp across the sky?

The Rings of Saturn

"Saturn is the planet of responsibility
and symbolized the ethic of hard work.
Under its influence a person's character
is strengthened through trial and difficulty."
Joanna Woolfolk

After seeing the rings of Saturn through binoculars
from a balmy bluff in Indian Summer,
the Milky Way's vast sweep of stars and nebulae,
the dusky dome where no city lights intrude,

after dreaming that we skated on the rings
of Saturn, red and black ice,
the celestial overpass, where no one honks;
in that unencumbered silence, it is enough

to wake, blue and ornery,
forget our daily affirmations,
have a second cup of hot black coffee
out of the old wheel thrown, ringed mug,

now chipped at the lip. Still,
it's speckled like the firmament,
and the coffee's good. Our daily fire.
It is enough to iron in the cold basement,

spray starch on cotton, glide
through domestic wrinkles, your bleached
white shirt which I prepare for you,
like bread, over and over.

It is enough to fold white underwear,
warm and soft as dough, this private ritual grown
through a quarter century of better or worse.
It is enough to find a ladybug

on the old wooden headboard
of the waterbed we refuse to give up,
and leave her there for luck. Well,
it's mostly better, isn't it?

We grow old skating under Saturn
making the most out of our blue, imperfect
planet, our blue, imperfect lives,
dismantling and remantling our dreams.

Voyagers 1 & 2. We distill, ironing
and pruning and changing our plans.
Yet in these rings of years, we keep the fire
of a life imagined well. The future swells

like stream from coffee mugs,
the ladybug flies, and our old handmade
wedding bands with gold and silver strata
carve their callous rings around our fingers.

At Three Arch Cape

Oceanside, Oregon. 7 a.m.
Low tide and empty beach.
Even the mist incandesces below
Three Arches, their peaks
like primitive gods. A faint rainbow
forms around them perfectly
like a shrine. Last week's measured life
with its compromises
like broken sand dollars, leaves.
On the great redwood's limb
now bleached bone-gray, our initials: CS/JS.
Who would guess a couple married
a quarter of a century, lapping
into the millennium? Still, today I walk alone,
head farther down my favorite inlet,
past the familiar shanties
and new condos rising: misguided
fortresses that trespass shifting dunes.
No matter what—I still return,
and when I round the bend to Netarts Bay,
the entire village, old and new,
is fodder for the fog pierced only by pelicans.
High hum of wind and gull's shriek.
Pelicans dipping. Today this beach
with its shells and parables is my companion,
and you, drinking coffee, reading newspapers.
You're earthbound. I'm tides and fog.
Only give me these dreamy mornings to keep.
Let me sit again on burnt driftwood,
my back against a dune, sing again the prayer
that ends with sanctus, sanctus.
The waves sizzle and stretch,
and I stretch too, arching upward,

arms open. Let the ferocious winds billow
under my big blue jacket, though I never quite
lift off. Who does? It is enough each year
to count myself among the lucky,
plucking perfect agates and holy ghost money
from sand, fill big pockets with grit.
And you in your blue stocking cap
and black leather jacket, waving.

Between Friends

Between Friends

Know that I'll soak up your words
like yeast in warm water, but don't

knead me dry. I'm as dependable
as a Rolex, but I too demand time.

Use me like a sieve, but no pebbles,
please. Play with me like a child would,

but catch the ball if I throw it back.
Fill me like a vase but shatter me

and your feet might bleed. Be as honest
as a tree dropping its leaves gently.

Surprise me but not with distance.
Let me steer when I'm upfront

and I promise that when it's your turn,
I won't be a backseat driver.

Take my gifts but put them in a closet
and Darling, I'm gone.

The Butterfly Tree

for Karla

Like monarchs returning to the Butterfly Tree,
large snowflakes sail past the window,

landing on the overgrown junipers.
Snow butterflies settling like sunshine.

I know a woman who lives where
a real Butterfly Tree grows sideways from a hill

near the San Andreas Fault, nearly wind-thrown.
Deep-rooted, it survives Pacific gusts, floods,

and even the earth swaying between its fingers
doesn't send it crashing. There each November

the monarchs return, awaited like the call
from a lover. Seduced by warm El Niño current,

they returned in droves, thick as snow this year.
Orange boughs. And when many died,

as butterflies may do, she took them in
and scattered them on her Christmas tree.

At this moment, it is January in Illinois.
A pair of cardinals search for juniper berries.

Their delicate talons leave soft calligraphy.
I knew a poet whose words were this graceful—

gossamer, lace wings of jazz and china.
She hit a tree—red berries on the snow,

which covers her now with a comforter
of snow butterflies. Crystal cape.

I know a man who can withstand an earthquake.
Geronimo winds cannot dislodge him.

How thoughtful that a tree grows farther down than up.
Spindly tangle, finger lace. Sometimes the enchanted

live with many spirits storming
in their hearts: butterfly, tree, cardinal . . .

Their roots must keep the hurricane at bay,
though branches dangle, and spines bend.

They flourish in fierce, jagged places,
eat the red, bitter berries, and mate for keeps,

yet fly on paper wings the baffling distance.

The Red Lacquer Room

for Lynda

We were hiding in The Red Lacquer Room,
the empty dance floor of the grand old Palmer House
deep in the center of Chicago, its black canyons,
dark skyscrapers, faint friction, sparks
of the El clambering like a craving. You said
I'd be surprised: how you'd lost your beauty.

Thin as a refuge, black and blue babushka twirled
into a turban high Bohemian style, you seemed
more like some ragged survivor than the gypsy
that you were. Dear Lynda, even when we dared
flick on the great white chandeliers
in The Red Lacquer Room, I knew the streets

had won but pretended we crouched together
in a lovely surreal dream where happy endings
bright as crystal chandeliers in ballrooms still glow.
I thought surely you'd find a way past
the city's chaos, jagged graffiti, pain of cracked
pavements, heels crushing, the stone souls.

I thought you might find stillness in the lake's
lapping tongues, a lilting gull, some small place
not quite as ecstasy. But no, you could never
be consoled by compromise, or live slowly
to keep and ending less violent, never fail
to see the long teeth behind the tongue.

Today I entered a store with delicious and sad surprises—
red lacquer boxes where gypsies and czarinas
dance in snow and fine horses with arched necks

bow their heads. I hold a red lacquer bowl,
deep wooden spoon, remember how you fed me
with your poems as fine as this red, glossy wood,

recall a recurring dream that really did come true:
I walked in the white arctic night
beneath the swirls of Saint Basil's, heels
gliding over the bricks of Red Square.
At that moment, I lost a world that could be measured
in square feet. You were there too.

The Empty Bowl

Water gathering in the round, granite bowl—
perhaps a thousand drops before it's full.
When the water crests the brim, it spills
from fullness. No place left to go but slip
down sides to the great earth that drinks it.

The bowl could contain, hold forever, moss
and stagnant waters murkier each year.
The bowl could dry from lack of tending
or simply scorch from sun and other forces
not within its keep. The bowl is deep

but something in it wants emptiness, the kind
Buddhists say is possible if only
you can stand the stillness long enough.
I hope I can. Today I say goodbye.
I am emptying this bowl, our friendship

algae-laden. I am scouring the bowl
and will not put it back where we found it
years ago when there was much to learn.
My cloth is gratitude, vinegar-wistful.
I've learned too late to move before the bowl

cracks, before its hurled, smashed to pieces.
Before the water's poisoned. Forgive me.
It's too late to make amends. We've slipped.
Charm's become annoyance. Interest...
boredom. Respect . . . tolerance . . . leaking, drying.

There's no more slack to cut. The bowl
wants emptiness, the round tabula rasa,
whatever floats us to the future. Loss
in a Chinese character is also opportunity.
Something in the bowl desires fresh water.

Canoe

At bow I paddle frantically
toward some imagined goal: an island

for our picnic, perhaps a heron's nest.
At stern you pop a beer, lean back,

expecting nothing but the day itself.
I shout commands, and your one

precision stroke means shooting rapids
or hanging on a rock. I am the eye.

You are the hand. Cross-legged,
scouting new territory, at different

speeds, we still keep center keel.
You keep me from capsizing. I keep you

from floating backward.

At the Grocery

Perhaps it's Pluto's transit
or a mild case of entropy
or maybe your eyes don't refuse to see
the old men bagging groceries
in January—
                           red knuckle grasping
at control, usefulness
this paper bag labeled Work Ethic
about to rip down the middle
while green-haired grandsons
wear ragged Bermudas in the snow
eat only food that requires no utensils
                           and whine
                           all the way to the mall.

Maybe it's Mercury in retrograde
or a terminal case of midlife crisis
or just some hot chocolate-covered
                           Karma
when your perfect summa cum laude friend
who's been married to Prince Charming
for twenty years dumps him for a frog
who's much more interesting
                           on his motorcycle.
She's wearing a black leather Harley Vest
and popping Rolling Rock into her cart.

It could be Neptune in the first house
or a major case of had-it-up-to-here
or just some hot creamy Goddess worship
when at least two
                           glory-of-god-and-motherhood

crones suddenly
       shear their hair
       shop together
       declare
that papaya looks luscious this time of year.

The Man at the Pool

The man with no legs swims today.
I see him lower himself from his wheelchair
into the pool, balancing on one hand at a time
like a Russian acrobat or Indian Yogi master.
The arms of Vulcan.
The torso of Zeus.
The body of a porpoise.
We must be the same age and I wonder
if he lost his legs in Viet Nam.
I have seen him many times here,
and he never looks depressed.
I love swimming with him,
in parallel lanes, how his porpoise-body
undulates, like an S on its back.
I love swimming with him
because he doesn't chop and slash
like so many other men
who send my measured crawl
slipping into the guard ribbon.
The porpoise-man glides by me easily
for I must pace myself to make
my 40 laps. At #22 I see him,
arms spread at the pool's rim.
Through fogged goggles,
the way he looks just then, I could imagine
the rest of his body, as powerful as his hands.
He holds a renegade straight-edge razor.
He says, "Look what I found in the pool."
I say, "What in God's name
is a razor doing in the pool?"
He says, "Gee. You think maybe
I should shave my legs?"

Masseuse

You have turned
my toes to velvet mushrooms,
my arches to cotton,
the balls of my feet to Indian drums,
my heels to onyx,
my ankles to pigeon feet,
my calves to oranges,
the back of my knees to creeks,
my knees to sleek creek stone,
my thighs to herons' necks outstretched,
my hip bones to eggs,
my lumbar to does' eyes,
the small of my back to an iceberg,
my spine to opal,
my shoulder blades to foothills,
my shoulders to satin ribbon,
the crimp of my neck to root,
my neck to stem,
my head to dandelion,
my hair to fluff—
scattered in the eucalyptus wind
of a late spring afternoon.

Smile Poem Found at the Bank

During a particularly difficult transaction
With a new young bank teller named Jason,
Who finds transferring funds
From savings to checking
A computer nightmare
For twenty minutes while the line gets longer
And agitated, and I have to resist
The thought that they are blaming me
So I must blame Jason,
I catch a sunbeam and chant to myself:
"All sentient beings seek happiness
And want to avoid suffering."
Something I catch myself thinking
A lot these days. Walking out,
I see a man who might be a customer
Or a derelict or Timothy Leary.
I try not to make eye contact,
But it's too late.
"I like your smile," he says.
"Thanks," I say,
For I am pathologically courteous
And unaware that I am smiling.
All these years I have wondered
Why strangers always and everywhere
Talk to me.
I worried: I must look like a sucker,
A loser, or worse—a person with no boundaries.
No standards, some wide vibe screaming,
"Please bug me. Bother me. Talk to me.
Whatever it is—you can tell me."
But today, today I learn that all along
It was just the friendly smile
I didn't even know I owned.

Before Grooming the Horse in Winter

She searches for old kernels with her nose
and finds them lodged within the burry spears.
She wants the bundled bales, but she's not close
enough behind the planks to reach the tiers.
A loose whinny drops her liquid muzzle,
and when Bruce the brown tomcat wraps his tail
around her fetlock, their noses nuzzle.
She rolls him. He jumps the highest bale.
Her icy tail whips against an old gray
plank, sets Bruce upon his haunches, but she
forgets their games, content to munch away.
Old Bruce won't have it, dives kamikaze.
They touch like willow branches in the barn
and speak a language I'm too fast to learn.

Virtues Revisited

A Friend Asks

Why I write poetry,
and though I've dreamed of this moment
for years, it still stops me
like a siren.
Because Mayan women do not weave chevrons
in desert sunset threads
because it is no longer useful.
Because the snowy egret leaves the marsh forever.
Because the people closest to me suffer.
Because words are bread.
Because writing it is mapless as driving back roads.
Because without it, my life is measured in paychecks.
Because I love you and can't tell you.
Because I couldn't stop even if I wanted to.
Because there are so many questions nobody asks.
Because someone wants to know.

The Dark Night Of the Soul

comes burning like a bullet—
fire-seed of knowledge—
tears down walls of denial,
leaves you staring into the blackest city
like Lot's wife
knowing you can never turn back;

comes when no pieces of the puzzle
called Your Life fit,
feels like a snake inside you.
My friend, I tell you there are choices
in your powerlessness,
if only you do not feed the snake.

I say: Give it nothing. No bread.
No words. No medicine or money.
Speak to no one who finds the snake
fascinating. Pay no one to charm it.
Beware of anyone
who says it can be tamed.

Sonnet For Live Words

Give me consonants snapping like snare drums,
the difference between a *t* and a *d*.
Serve me a whole slice of bread, not just crumbs.
A tangerine's not a dromedary.
Speak vowels tunnel-shaped or sharp as skate blades.
Send me sentences that flow from the top
of the mountain, then roar over cascades.
Let them shout clear and frothy 'til they stop
for commas, rocks and pebbles that protect
the stream from gushing. Please, say what you mean.
Words, like water, can become polluted
too. Think of language, a gift crisp and clean.
Long for great, live words to reel in like fish.
Fry them up, digest them, and be nourished.

Opportunity

        doesn't knock.
It accumulates
the same way riches do:
        the more you have,
the more you get.

Opportunity is a gaggle
of geese resting
        on the river's edge:
        they know what to do
and do it. Opportunity
        is a velvet box
filled with lottery tickets
that read Yes, yes, yes,
stashed for twenty years,
        cashed in
on a whim or mimsy day.

Opportunity is a paper
        or risks
blown wide, then popped
and dropped, like confetti
on your life's parade.

        It's the walking stick—
carved, notched, and grooved—
with a handle
you remember to grasp
past each panicked precipice,
each ragged rock,
every rugged, renegade vista.

It's a basket filled with fruit—
pear, papaya, pomegranate, apple—
    sweet knowledge
the paradise we leave behind.

Point of Departure

When the last train trembles
       silent in its tracks
and the telephone's ring becomes
       its whistle
or a lone gull's cry
                        go
where you can be smaller
       than a hummingbird's egg,
or where you can dance
       anonymous in purple socks.

Wear a cape with stars sewn on,
       a periwinkle ascot
and unbecoming bi-focals. In fact,
       unbecome altogether.
                     Unbecome
the brown and black jackets
       hung straight
these working years. Unbecome
       your dreams of pencils,
black coffee, tests already passed.

Let loose
       the leather leash of approval.
Bark at anyone
       who insists you heel.
                     Bite
the hand that feeds you.

Four Virtues Revisited

Patience was the well filled with cool, clear water,
the well you dipped your bucket in and drank deeply.

Now the water's muddy, the bucket crashes.
It leaks and comes up empty.

Ambition was the train you road to work
and points beyond: Rome, Paris, Montego Bay . . .

You loved its noisy juggle, its lurches, screeching
halts, every stranger and view along the way.

Now the train's a rickety hassle, rude passengers
who talk too much, too may stops, no real destination.

Compromise was the rack you hung your coat on,
changing with each season's barometric shifts.

Now you're old and nicked.
You could use some tender restoration.

Work was the sharp pencil that defined you
until you reached the last sheet of gleaming graph paper.

Now you long for solitude, silence of delicious nothing,
hours that glide as gracefully as winter swans.

Meandering

After a lifetime of goals and plans and straights lines,
you might love the taste of meandering,
the sweet champagne of it,
the swirls and curves,
sheer movement,
mellow loam.
      It might be enough to meander like the creek,
roll over round, speckled rocks and carp,
past an old black man's bucket,
bubble over levees,
under bridges,
waving
      at trolls, prairie-grass tassels, cat-tails,
wild iris and wood lilies. It
might be enough to let
old dreams turn to
mud that feeds
      who-know-what creatures of the creek—
perhaps the sand crane or snowy egret—
spreading yourself thin, floating
downstream. After naming
each couched desire,
every ambition
      turned to silt, the curly algae of disappointment,
the general muck of getting wherever
it was you thought you had to go,
let the banks of the creek
embrace you like
a lover
      absolved of any erosion that might come
between you, yes. It is enough
to flow and trickle
and lilt at last—
           the sheer unstuck
              meandering.

Whimsical Meditation on Power

Power is like an old Porsche 911,
a ladybug on the outside,
a panther on the inside,
gets going best in fifth gear
zooming down the Autobahn of Life.

      It's the black definition
in a Peña painting, the jawbone
of an Indian woman,
      her onyx bowl.

      Power is the mum
that makes it through the fall frost,
bursting purple, yellow, russet
along the white garage.

Power is the woman in charge
      of her own life, the woman
who's given her ragged victim's shawl
to Goodwill, burned
her little black Dictionary of Resentments,

      bought a periwinkle poncho
woven in soft, silk threads,
stopped talking on the telephone
and gave up her jealousy for Lent.

      Power is the water refusing
to get stuck, the water leaving
all the jagged rocks behind.

Remembering a Line by Stanley Kunitz

"I only borrowed this dust."

Today a slant of southern sun
Settles on my neck, beams
On the young white dog sniffing
Junipers in the neighbor's yard.
I did not waste my youth
With its wild and dangerous bends,
Its terrible lovers and huge mistakes.
I regret not one saltlick of it.
       It has brought me to this evergreen
Resolution, like the blue spruce
When it glistens with frost.
I came by stillness slowly
Like the river near a dam,
Like the silent syncopation
Of a slow jazz rift blown
By Miles Davis on a rainy day,
Like the snow that feeds black soil.
       This day the sunset maple's small,
Veined leaves burnish crimson,
Pumpkin-orange, and ox-blood.
Though it's quite illegal here,
I swear I smell burning leaves
Like old bishops' benedictions.
It's my fifty-third birthday: 11-7-49.
All numbers odd, like me.
I can't quite call it zeal, but
I'm grateful for this even keel.

Embrace Uncertainty as a Cloud

When uncertainty hangs humid
    Thick as a steel-gray sky
And you can't tell if a storm hovers
    In the charcoal clouds
Or if only a gentle Zen rain will follow,
    Return to that still, quiet place.
Imagine you are the water itself,
    The deep center of a blue, glacial lake,
The sizzling tide pulled back to its source.
    Know that whatever rain must come
Has its purpose if you wish to find it.
    The rain takes many forms, gathering
Its legions with the wind, which might be
    Sweet summer breezes or wind sheer
Pulling pines and locust from their roots.
    Embrace uncertainty as a cloud holding water,
Building its cumulous castles in the stratosphere,
    Until release comes, and come it will.

Poem to My Retirement

I love the Zen of you:
contentment in cleaning a closet
satin-finished joy of painting a door
green pleasure of singing evensong
deep spell of reading hardbound library books
sheer greed of writing poetry on call.

I love your slow, graceful pace:
tinkering with tarnished brass
painting an archway periwinkle
sorting out clothes I'll never need to wear
wearing only comfortable cottons
planning a trip without mania.

I love the way you flow like water:
meandering through rooms with new eyes
converging at a desk where stacked books beckon
dripping like fresh coffee, my morning's transfusion
crashing on the telemarketer who disrupts my reverie
saying No without a second guess.

I love your loosening the knots of anxiety:
sleep's not an acrobat turning cartwheels
mornings not a gaggle of pantyhose with holes
lunch's not a microwave within stale, stifled walls
afternoon's not a cardboard office
evenings not collapse time in front of re-runs.

I dig your reaping of renegade seeds:
patience to listen to an old aunt's story
delicious interest of wise investments
sweet voice reaching a four-octave range
kooky, bad novella finished and shelved
speaking Italian *pui bene. Si. Bellisima?*

I love the way one thing leads to another:
a nudge becomes a poem
a phone call becomes a scheme
a color becomes a new room
a spice becomes a fest
a book an odyssey.

Tiger Wing

Fear's the fierce tiger
with claws curled,
but courage
is not the whip unfurled,
nor the cage.
A quiet voice tames the rage.
Faith is a wing or oiled lock,
a wild iris growing
from forever rock.
A cage with rusty lock
is comforting
to anyone with broken wing,
but broken wings must mend
and from cage doors ascend
perhaps a winged tiger.

Sometimes the Body

Dream Bandits

Sometimes the body is an inmate
who never forgets

how every hair is numbered. Yet,
before sleep, it may recall

sweet fire of careless ecstasy.
On such nights, it might wake

to full moons and raccoons
cavorting on the skylight.

Then follow your body
to that puddle of moonlight.

Lie under stars. Watch dream bandits
bite each other's necks, stretch

toward the wicked moon. Press
your fingers to the pane.

Let the small, black hands scratch back,
mere shaft of plexiglass between you.

Food

I have feasted on the world's delicacies:
caviar in Kiev, lobster in Bar Harbor,
high tea at the Ritz, artichokes in Monaco,
scallops in Digby, raclette in the Valais,
paella in Barcelona, dolmades in Athens,
clam linguini in Venice, chicken mole in Oaxaca . . .
Shall I go on?
I celebrate what I've taken in of the world—
more than my fair share—
and I am more than satisfied.

Now I want simple food:
crusty bread with homemade raspberry jam,
raw cashews and dried papaya,
polenta, plain with a dash of fresh Romano,
vegetable soup with cilantro, mint tea with honey,
fresh apple muffins—not too big . . .
Need I say more?
I celebrate what I take in this world—
my fair share—
I celebrate simply and am satisfied.

When Less Is More

Today an amazing machine
says my body needs 1447 calories
per day to run efficiently.
Any more turns to fat
which makes me look
like a koala bear. Of course
I love koala bears
and one could do worse,
but that's not the point.
At fifty-two, my body needs
       less. I need
           less. Mostly I love
the elegant simplicity
this time can bring if you
remove the clutter.
       Yes. Postmenopausal zeal
          is real.
I am a woman glad
the last Modess box gathers dust
like the Monopoly game
with missing pieces. Glad
to dance off the clanky, hardscrabble
festival of desire and striving,
striving,
like spider who can't stop
spinning webs
where they're sure to be
unwanted. Happy, yes,
for a life pared
to the succulent essentials
and time around each one
       to savor. Like

radio jazz on a cold, February night
beneath a blue comforter,
        listening
with no worry of morning's rush,
no pantyhose to bind you,
no boss to defer to.

Like that
and the watermelon relish
of a life pointed towards exquisite
        freedom, O.

Choosing less to have more.
Debt-free. Unencumbered
by mortgage, greed,
        the need to please.
My suitcase is small and worn,
its badges, wounds healed.
Let us celebrate
the great dismantling
of all indentured servitude.
Now even the body reaches for this—
        less bulk, more nourishment.
                Nothing to waste.

This Mild Winter Day

Late Sunday afternoon. January 11.
Today river ice clots. Little platelets
still snake unpredictably
near the river's edge. Few people,
this mild winter day,
dimly blue as the worn ceilings
of Italian chapels. The sun steadfast
white over the bridge.

                    It's 2004, and I'm glad.
Not that 2003 was bad. Just
that is felt like the year I lived
with a manic-depressive lover: When
it was good, more than your tiny, tiny curl
stood on end: When it was bad,
it was like last summer's wind sheer,
the tornado sky that severed and sliced
a thousand locusts, and swirled pine roots
from their homes for keeps.

                    In 2003, I visited
a friend in Georgia, anticipating the annual
female ritual with verve: the conch cottage
at Tybee Island, the Atlantic's warm massage,
bursts of Southern molasses sun,
frozen margaritas and the deep sleep
of friendship. Instead riptides lined the shore.
The water was a witch's brew:
turbulent sand, ragged shells that stung
our backs, an overkill of jellyfish.
The humidity resurrected winter ghosts
of the arthritis we weren't ready
to admit we have. In 2003, I began to grow
old.

                    But here along the river,

this mild winter day, only ducks break
the stillness. A splash of snow
still clings to grass blades like
all those coincidences that guide us
to our bruised but brilliant incompletions.
And now, this very moment,
when I need it most, I stop to see
a word some renegade has painted
on the path. There in mustard yellow:
HOPE, with an arrow pointing forward.

Nevertheless

Brutal wind gashes the rafters
of the neglected house owned by the landlord
who eats money for breakfast; nevertheless,
a pair of regal pigeons find deep shelter
in the rafters' darkest recesses, raise
nestfuls of fledglings month after month.
The threat of anthrax spreads like gossip,
tears with its jagged teeth and pointed tongue,
scares us with its kernel of truth.
The country goes from Highest Alert
to Highest Highest Alert, which proves that
superlatives can be squared; nevertheless,
all over blue and white-collar neighborhoods
men and women pound nails into new roofs:
rustic cedar, forest green, slate blue, and pewter gray.
If this isn't hope, what is?

A middle-aged woman sees a stranger
in the full-length mirror, licks her losses
like wounds; nevertheless,
she's astonished to find them healed
if not quite invisible, finds herself gratefully
unburdened and unhurried, finds it keen:
the mortgage is dismantled,
her days are unencumbered
by youth's whirling dervish of wants,
finds she's still dancing, slow and graceful
on peaceful mornings all her own,
knows she's kept her promises.
And though she knows "Eventually"
probably came and went, she's still swimming
in the tiled pool of her dreams,
which for the most part have come true.
She sings a song of charity and passion.
If this isn't faith, what is?

Sparrows Falling From the Sky

A Remembrance For Panajachel

Guatemala, 1978

They tell me you have been ravaged,
Mayan Mother. Small bones crushed
by guerillas and earthquakes.

Your small son wears the black band
over the sleeve of the perfect shirt
you wove for him in ancient Mayan red.

Lake Atitlan is bluer than tears,
where sulfur springs are tinged
with Mayan blood. Even the poinsettias

bleed when no one picks the coffee beans
and avocados rot in the jungle.
Did they burn your thatched roofs?

Do heads of slaughtered chickens still
lie beside your novena's candle?
Do you pray to Quetzalcoatl, Guadalupe, Castro?

Or did the earth mercifully swallow you?
I swear by the cloth I bought from you,
Little One, I did not imagine happiness

in your black diamond eyes. Your life,
three thousand years rich, was no poorer
than mine. Who will buy your chevroned weavings?

Oppenheimer, After Forty Years

The Seattle Post-Intelligencer, June 16, 1985

I cannot get beyond the face in the photo.
Are the large, languid eyes blue
like a clear desert sky?
Are they the pale amber of grain?
Or have they burned
into the color of dust?
There is a wide gap between the brows,
a space large enough for a third eye.
The eyes do not seem mad,
or brilliant.
but if I look close enough,
is that the radiance of a thousand tears?
The eyes are human
and the rest of the face is lean and polished,
waxy and pale like a cancer victim's.
There is little flesh.
Does this man live on thought
or particles of air,
like those in a secret Indian sect?

> At the instant of detonation, he recalled
> fragments from the BHAGAVAD-GITA:
> > If the radiance of a thousand suns
> > Were to burst at once into the sky,
> > That would be like the splendor
> > of the Mighty One . . .
> > I am become Death,
> > The destroyer of worlds.

The ears are small and pointed like an otter's,
There is no flesh on the lobe.
The cheekbones are low and delicate.
There is no peasantry here,
The lips are small and still.

He is lighting a curved black pipe-
a prized possession?
The match burns into a small trinity,
lit by his huge, incongruous hands,
hands you wouldn't run from if the frame were large,
hands, mottled like trout,
that have a life outside the mind,

hands that light the furnace of the world.

The early Spaniards called this region
of wind and distance Jornada del Muerto,
Journey of Death, or the Route of the
Dead Man. Oppenheimer had been reading
John Donne's holy sonnets:

Batter my heart, three-personed God; for you
As yet but knock, breathe, and seek to mend.

"Trinity, we'll call it Trinity," he said.

The chin and the forehead are regular;
they are not strong.
There is nothing wrong in the face.
No hint of deformity.
No extra skin,
though the Adam's Apple is sharp
and the neck skin seems red and radiated.
The thin, white hair is closely cropped
though not military or machismo.
The entire body seems to lean forward
as if there was another large hand on the shoulder.

And the beast slouches toward Bethlehem.

Epiphany

Moscow, January, 1991

At last the snow that covers the bricks
of Red Square is not tinged with blood,
and the myriad footprints become one
straight line or great circle,
not phantom shadows frozen
in January's white night, massacred
or starved. No longer hungry for flesh,
the bear begins her true journey now,
free to tread the tundra,
play in the snow, wrapped
only in her great, long-awaited spirit.

The people walk with God,
who hid in the swirls of Saint Basil's,
who cried from the souls of the dead,
who lived in Chagall's paintings.
who occupied servants' quarters
in the Hermitage,
who spoke in Nureyev's leaps,
who placed a mark upon the forehead
of the peacemakers,
who waits and works all slow miracles.

Because twenty years ago I
walked in Red Square, stood in long lines
to see Lenin's corpse, or buy one orange,
because I too know the disappointment
of too much thought and theory
and have found church doors locked
in my own country, because I wait
as the eagle dies in the dessert,
I must proclaim this epiphany
with bells. I am burdened,

bundled in a heavy black coat,
a bright flowered babushka. Never
has the Artic night been so white:
Thousands of candles cupped
by hands too used to cold.
The words of the carols are difficult,
buried so long in ice,
thawing now, thawing,
seeping like blood
into the earth, which has no choice
but to bear.

How the Road Saved Us

September, 2001

Ten days after watching, seared
by pyrotechnical horror of the Twin Towers' spines,
each vertebrae sliding down like dominoes,
the surreal crematory of American dream—
we finally yank ourselves away
from that black hole we've been sucked into,
finally say, "No TV today.
Let's take a ride." Let's escape.

Let's go into the womb of the old Porsche
we've named Ice-Blue Cool
for its rare glaze, soft as a jazz rift
blown by Sonny Rollins on a good day.
It's cold but sunny in the Midwest.
A crisp September morning.
Whir of sunroof, chirp of radar detector,

a few vintage cassettes, and we agree:
"No radio. No news today."
No news. Just Highway 81.
Just Green County, Wisconsin, past Monroe
where we buy brown, 9-grain bread,
a few peaches and plums,
a tiny pumpkin from the farmer's market,
the air still ripe with harvest.

We eat a Swiss cheese sandwich
at Baumgartner's, where the old proprietor
seems dazed, mistake-laden,
confusing orders left and right.
Business as usual. But not quite.
We're headed to New Glarus
but get to Argyle instead, a tiny town
with a wheat-colored clapboard hotel,

old wooden stairs entangled with late blooming
rose climbers, renegade sweet pea,
a gaggle of weeds, and old farm wives
eating slices of pie with cheddar cheese
or vanilla ice cream. Old farm wives
talking of arthritis and medication.
We take a pee
and head down County C,

knowing we've somehow lost our way,
going in some obelisk direction,
the way I remember D.C., its street names
sometimes changing at rush hour.
We've lost our way
but there's beauty all around us:
red and white Wisconsin barns,
shutters and stone foundations a century old,

sumac turning soft crimson,
a few pumpkin-colored maples,
purple phlox and goldenrod.
prairie grass and cat tails.
Now and then a hawk perches
on a fence or telephone wire,
a monarch makes it across the road,
skunk smell taints the clover.

The hay, round bales like large bread loaves,
grace the Kettle Morraine, here
on the road, the road that saves us, here
in Green County, Wisconsin, where
it is still possible to say: Bread Basket of the World,
still possible to know how large the land is,
its quaint hills and silos beckoning,
a prayer in fifth gear edging 'round the sweeper.

Letter to John Lennon

on his birthday, October 8, 2001

Dear John,
The radio just played "In My Life,"
my favorite of all your songs.
I'm at my desk under a skylight,
a blustery battleship blue sky in its dome,
an October slash of sun on my shoulder
like a ghost.
                Let me try to tell you how
it's been these last four weeks,
though I'm sure you know.
                I believe
for me it began with a coal-black dream
in summer: the blackest blanket of sky
settled like a plague. Thick tornados
loomed like pillars on a confusing horizon.
People ran helter skelter.
                A bad dream
in a time of relative bliss, a bad dream
too lucid to shake off, like acid reflux
clinging to your throat in the middle of the night.
The summer had its sorrow: A cousin died.
A friend's father.
                I waited for the third
in the superstitious trinity of sorrows.

A balmy morning, September 11,
the fragrance of concord grapes ripening,
the lick of September's lemon tongue.
I'm sucking sour skins off grapes,
tasting the gelatin burst,
spitting out the woody seeds, watching
a cardinal waiting for his turn.
A simple, languorous Midwest morning
like the kind you might remember,
John, with your aunt at a cozy English cottage.

82

The phone rang, its tenor menacing
as a siren: My husband telling me
to turn on the news.

The rest Yoko must have told you:
Passenger jets slicing the torso
of the World Trade Towers,
stabbing into its belly,
ripping out its guts.
The pentagon
       blazing.
       The cry of holy war
       the most unholy of all
       war.

       First we carried
       it in our bodies:

Eyes burned. Muscles burdened, stiff.
Headaches. Shaking hands. Heartburn.
We said Business as usual
       but we felt it
in our bones, heavy with uncertainty.
Grief brought out our best and worst.
Rage whipped our backs
when we least expected: in grocery lines,
at banks, during dinner, on boats.
Some of us argued about the color of paint.
Some of us needed to be alone
but couldn't be.
Some of us made bread, gave money,
tried to sing.
Some of us became village idiots.
Jerry Falwell blamed the gays.
Rush Limbaugh went deaf.
I lost my patience

83

and couldn't get it back.
Some thought banning pocketknives
or checking IDs would help.

John, I'm singing
"Everything's gonna be all right,"
but this is no magical mystery tour
though sometimes the earth and sky
still remember us: I saw a rainbow in the East
and tawny Mars gleaming in the South
with Mercury beneath it like a semi-colon.
Last night I dreamed a swarthy man
drove a black truck down a gravel road,
made a U-turn near the horizon,
then plowed his truck into my brick house,
which mercifully kept standing.
                              Except
suddenly the man is at my window
behind gauze curtains.
                        He has no eyes,
just holes like Oedipus. John,
all I am saying is
we gave peace a chance. You
might be pleased at how far we have come.
I'd like to sing "Imagine there's no heaven"
over and over.
                  I'd like to drop it into
all the cells of hate, like anthrax slipped
into an envelope. And John,
it's the craziest damn war.
We're dropping food along with bombs.

An Eagle Poem Found February, 2002

There he was, an old eagle, encaged
that winter day at Atwood Forest Preserve.
A wounded eagle, taken in by park rangers,
to live the rest of his life by the mercy
of kind attendants who feed him small, furry
road-kill still fresh enough to eat.
As I approached softly on the light snow,
the eagle let out high, staccato cries
like a round of gunfire, then turned my way.
I saw his missing eye, half his head caved in—
the work of humans I am told. If
at this moment my country were not
shouting its own war cries, wrapping
its huge talons around lesser prey;
I might have thought
only this: Poor Eagle, who will not fly again,
will not resume your eagle's way. O formidable
bird of prey, vulture king once
soaring over the Rock and Kishwaukee rivers,
no silver-brown fresh fish will glint
from your beak, swept to your nest
where your gossamer-tufted children feed.

To Love My Country

To love my country is to say No:
No to the long commute in a vehicle
that makes us depend on foreign oil
or the destruction of God's last country.
No to the starter castle planted on Illinois'
black earth, the most fertile in the world.
No to mindless medicalization
that most of us don't need and cannot afford.
No the unnecessary slaughter of trees.
No to the cell phone, call waiting, and telemarketer.
No to phony political correctness
that creates yet another set of chains.
No to fast food
eaten without utensils.
No to violent pornography
and lyrics that kill.
No to more noise and distraction.
No to the endless labeling of children.
No to mindless procreation.
No to cruelty to children in any form.
No to cruelty to animals everywhere.
No to the National Inquirer.
No to religious hypocrisy that brings
no peace, and those who insist we use it.
No to face lifts, tattoos, and the endless
tweaking of our sentient bodies.
No to corporate greed
for it always causes suffering.
No to rudeness and the temptation
to become uncivil and unkind.
No to living beyond our means, sleep walking
in a capitalist dream gone haywire.

To love my country is to say Yes:
Yes to the gas efficient vehicle.
Yes to living in the community
where we work, and supporting it.
Yes to the wilderness within it.
Yes to reasonable health and medical care.
Yes to the redwoods, pines, oaks, and rubber tree.
Yes to the rain forest and mountain laurel.
Yes to the machines that free us
not distract or complicate us.
Yes to the soulfulness of Thomas Moore
and the gentleness of Lisel Mueller.
Yes to the Return to the Garden
and the fragrance of lilies and lilacs.
Yes to truly free and unencumbered thought.
Yes to fresh food thoughtfully prepared
and Mom and Pop diners in small towns.
Yes to Cassandra Wilson, Paul McCartney,
Aretha Franklin, Charlotte Church, Debussy
and all music that elevates.
Yes to good parenting.
Yes to children playing in zoos, museums,
parks, beaches, and safe playgrounds.
Yes to children on bikes and with kites.
Yes to manatees, whales, owls, tigers,
dolphins, eagles, and cabbage moths.
Yes to taking in stray dogs and cats.
Yes to using library cards.
Yes to feeding the homeless.
Yes to celebrating face and body
grown rugged and interesting with age.
Yes to strolling out of the fast lane.
Yes to finding your bliss
even if the money doesn't come.
Yes to living the perfectly simple, abundant
American dream, which is truly within our means
if only we open our eyes and stay awake.

The Tree Trimmers

Their huge orange trucks bellow in
like Sherman tanks,
brakes squealing like pigs to slaughter.
Then the groan and whine,
the sawing off of leafy maple limbs,
speckled sycamore,
a squirrels' nest crashing to black pavement.
All morning the menacing moan and buzz,
crack and fury of ancient trees,
trees as old as the great turtles of the Yucatan,
old enough to have their guts ripped out
in the name of delicacy or safety,
as fanatical as ethnic cleansing.
One truck clumsily slides in front
of my house, my old bungalow
in this old neighborhood, chosen
for its old Norway maples, oaks, and poplars,
its blue spruce, magnolias, and sycamore—
not for the prestige of new faux palaces
in prairies and farmland.
My yellow maple is huge and full,
round and heavy like the Laughing Buddha
I try to summon in my heart but can't:
I'm attached to the outcome:
I want to save my tree
again this year because someone
with sawdust for brains
and a big contract with Com Ed
decreed that trees pose problems:
they combust, cause power failures,
entreat wires to zap them.
I've been here thirty years

and long to witness such amazing feats
by trees. Has this plague simply skipped me
like the Passover? I ask the trimmer
who's flicking his cigarette butt
in my driveway which he's blocking, "If you were
the wind, would you have more fun flapping
wires in gaping holes or trembling in small spaces?"
He thinks I'm the madwoman of 13th Avenue.
I tell him, "This is the Midwest. We don't
have mountains or ocean, just trees.
Did you know we were once called the Forest City?"
He says, "Well you've got the river."
I say, "Well, I don't live on the river."
He's sure I'm the madwoman of 13th Avenue
when suddenly it rains.
He's sheltered by the tree
but misses the irony of this.
The men spend the rest of the day
drinking coffee, smoking, and waiting
for orders from Com Ed. They tell me
they'll be back first thing tomorrow.
It's a perfectly beautiful day.
I've waited for three hours
for the trucks to arrive. It's mid-morning.
No tree trimmers.
I'm saying the Serenity Prayer.
It isn't working.
I have appointments to keep
but am afraid of what I'll find when I get home.
Darlings, when did we let someone
name trees enemies? When did this sea
of mangled leaves and butchered woods
become preferable to a solo mishap
so unlikely you'd have to be a vigilante
to witness it—a tree throwing off sparks,

electrocuting everyone who chanced being in it
for that few minutes when the wind roared
through the middle of the tree
in the middle of the night, a problem
as easily solved by resetting a clock
or turning off a computer?

Sparrows Falling from the Sky

The soprano, whose voice is brilliant
As fire, sings the aria from Madam Butterfly
On the radio in the Port Townsend Antique Store.

The notes build like snow before an avalanche
On Mount Baker across the bay.
This could be heaven, I am thinking

Examining the quirky Nippon vases
I have grown fond of: the ardor of their attempts
At European Baroque foiled

By the ever-graceful elongated necks
Of snow geese, the calligraphy of stylized trees.
How I love this upstart marriage of East and West.

The aria reaches its zenith when I enter
Booth #23, a dark cove devoted to things Nippon:
The era before Pearl Harbor,

Before the high society ladies scratched off
Nippon from the bottom of tea sets
Delicate and filigreed as small, old hands.

The aria reaches its zenith, which
Would have been enough to fog my glasses,
Enough to flood my eyes. But

There on the wall a strange painting
Startles me. It is so topsy-turvy, so unidealized
I have to get closer to it to see what gives.

A cacophony of bird wings, helter-skelter
Like a firestorm, in faded red and muddy
Charcoal. Birds adrift like autumn leaves.

It reads: Sparrows Falling from the Sky.
Hiroshima. Circa 1900. Artist Unknown.
It grips me by the throat—rain on my face.

The Grace Of the
Gentle Unambitious

Morning In Moscow, 1969

Icy wind on white knuckles.
Black coat huddling at bus stop.
No one talks.

The bus arrives,
painted lukewarm, hissing carbon
the same color as the air.

They tell me it is free.
Yet squeezed among dark shoulders
I am shoved up steps

to the old woman
who nods and rings paper kopecks
for some Russian purpose.

Another old woman sweeps
that state's street with a pine branch broom.
Her heavy black coat

makes a small shadow
against Saint Basil's Cathedral.
Even her babushka dims

in the incongruous swirls
of this giant's turban.
It is still white night.

I walk alone in Red Square.
I sink, dizzy,
into this red cobblestone lake,

the sanctioned blood of murders
beneath my feet, know
why there are so few Russian men.

Lenin, the Great Comrade, is still
preserved: A line of chafed, inscrutable faces
wait as though awaiting bread.

I watch the children whose fur caps
reincarnate a time when red
was the color of children's faces,

decorated tunics and Cossack sashes,
the fires they danced around.
Now, no trees break the bitterness

of this cutting snow.

Lines Written for Charlotte in Bronte Country

"I see at intervals a cage; a vivid, restless captive is
there; were it but free, it would soar cloud-high."
Rochester, *Jane Eyre*

No forest breaks the bony wind settling
like a skeleton in the moors and hearths
in Yorkshire. Winter seeps into small bones
where brownstone houses creak like old mastiffs.
Cuttleboned, sharpened in this loving cage,
you stayed within the Haworth parsonage
until you woke like a hummingbird and flew
above the phlox that sway in greening moors.
Though the yarrow's fragrant in these rocky
crannies, still the landscape broods. Shadows
still cover the fields like ghosts, hovering.

Pear Blossoms

Rain on attic dormers,
Debussy,
and pear blossoms bursting
outside my window
like the string of fireworks
exploding on Chinese New Year
in the Lahaina twilight.
Mixture of sulfur, sea salt,
plumeria to know Tai Chi
with a lithe Japanese woman
full of fervor, a tiny guru
in billowing white.
                                Wistful,
I wondered what it would be
to be her, living
a life so deliberately sacred
every move connects and balances.
Perfect Yin and Yang.

Rain quiet on the roof,
open window, cardinal calling
and pear blossoms breeching
like the whales of Kaanapali Bay
that perfect February day
in the Year of the Golden Dragon
in the Year of Our Lord 2000.
post-millennium madness,
in which no Apocalypse blew in
to destroy us all.
                        Instead
potion of Kona coffee, papaya,
squeeze of lime there on the lanai
the folds of Molokai's mountains

with its secret anguish of lepers
long gone, here in paradise
where whales spout,
their victorious tails graceful
as calligraphic Vs.

April bellows though attic windows,
thunder,
and the pear blossoms I've waited for
all year unfurl.
        Edenic, the garden I remember
on the road to Haleakala. Eucalyptus.
The crater's chasm large as longing,
dry as desire. Alone
that night I floated on my back
in an egg-shaped pool, enclosed
by rows of dark hibiscus.
                        The moon
was a gypsy's earring studded
by Saturn and Jupiter, conjoined diamonds
growing ever closer like a new paradigm.

            No one witnessed
this epiphany that buoys me through
this vast and sacred year,
a year where solitude is my dearest
and most deliberate companion,
and private rituals open like pear blossoms.

Paris on $5/Day X 2 / 1973

A thin Tunisian man served breakfast
at the pensione near Gare du Nord:
the heavy pitcher of black, rich coffee;
real cream, 4 huge croissants,
slab of sweet, white butter;
petite tub of orange marmalade—
atop white paper lace on an orange tray.
We ate on a slim balcony
between open shutters that day,
our first in Paris.
            Of course,
we were compelled to pack in
perennial tourist pleasures:
the Louvre, famous fountains
whose names we no longer recall,
a stroll to the Eiffel Tower,
content in our vow of poverty
to let others ride the elevator, thanks.
We lit slender candles in Notre Dame,
sat on the Seine's bank near a boat
with black sails.
            Dinner was a late picnic
of cheap wine, bread and cheese
at a bench beneath the honeycomb dome
of Sacre Coeur. We walked and walked
down streets and alleys of no significance
except to us, bodies light and bristling with pheromones,
the jet fuel of desire,
the electric hunger of the world
stretching out ahead.
            Because
we didn't give a damn about so many things
yet, because we didn't have to, we spent

less than $5 each before we crashed
at the pensione, slept with the shutters wide open,
didn't mind the smoky Parisian night at all,
most likely dreamed of trains and strangers.

Mira Makes it to Samos

Mira rides a rented cycle, carries
        goatskins filled with wine, fresh figs
                and feta in a net, and searches for something

she'll never find in any theory.
        An old man passes, sideways on a donkey,
                worry-beads and tassels jangling. He knows

Pythagoras once walked, arms clasped,
        beneath these olive trees, but doesn't care,
                and nearing Hera's Temple, he won't even blink.

He's off to play pinochle, shuffle
        cards, drink red wine in stocky glasses,
                and let the sun melt the blood in his hands.

He's forgotten the fervent young teacher—
        a second cousin?—who told
                wide-eyed children their island's history,

forgotten the Allies watching
        from white-washed walls of bougainvillea.
                He'll boast about his nephew. Tassos Theoharris,

a Somebody in America, where
        every myth comes true. Who'll tell
                him that it's Tom Harris now, or that

the gods have been demoted
        from Management to Sales, proper
                nouns to vulgar verbs: midasize, vulcanize…

where even Venus might arrive

in blue jeans? Still, there goes Mira,
        saluting him as though she'd found Atlantis.

Her Kawasaki whines and strains,
        winding a terrain so rocky, a road
                so thin, she'll have to walk.

In those tempered ruins,
        she'll lift her wine sack as if to toast
                whatever gods have brought her here.

Fort Zachary Beach, Key West

It's a place we return to in January
(the cruelest of months)
not for its vast Floridian beaches
(there are none here)
laden with oiled beauties
or fine pink sand

but for its gentle slopes
the mingling salt waters
of the Gulf and the Atlantic
the nudge of Cuba
                90 miles away.
The wind was brisk but nothing
like the chill we thought we left
behind
        (we didn't). The sky
was Key West bright
and white sails fluttered
a stone's throw away, when

a young man walked by, specter-thin
and yellow-skinned
his head bound by a white scarf
that beat
        like a gull's wing on the updraft.

AIDS we said together
before a seaweed tangle of thoughts
rose from remission in our minds.
He
        looked like a refugee
poor soldier of misfortune
like a nun martyred for love.

We
        wanted him walk
        on water.

At the Train Station

After Staying with Family in Bologna

When he kisses her, you can see the sign
      behind his back: Vota Comunista—
peeling like the bleached skin of the buildings.

The shutters are so old that they careen
      against the sun-baked plaster of the walls,
where laundry waves like flags and slaps the sky.

When the train came wailing into the station,
      I thought I could ride it anywhere for more
of this—this jazz of laughter in cafes,

this grace of the gentle unambitious. Yet
      I wonder what it really would have meant
to live a lifetime in these flats, cooking

and sewing, eating and sleeping,
      a cotton apron pinned against my breast,
a wooden rolling pin that rails the dough

a hundred-thousand times. Porco Miseria!
      A light percussive shadow on all things,
a beat that really knows no jazz at all.

Marin Muse

Mount Tamalpais, how the golden mist
　　　gathers around your slopes.
Blink of deer. Bay glimmer. Memories
　　　of bridges that vanish in fog.
They call you the Sleeping Maiden.
　　　Dreamer of potent dreams:
atomic tangerine sun. Green drum
　　　beating at sunset, golden
coin floating on the horizon, ocean
　　　medallion. Pacific blue.
Roar of surf at Stinson Beach, hot
　　　lovers, toes sand-scorched,
Sand angels mingled in the dune.

Let us breath, let us taste, let us eat
　　　hot raspberry crisp, here
at the Bolinas Bakery, where time
　　　took so many downers
and smoked so much sweet weed,
　　　even the dogs are stoned.
They sleep all day in the shade,
　　　think gray dog-thoughts:
To scratch a flea or not? Not. Not
　　　the 70's, 80's, 90's. Not
the roadside sign. Beware you
　　　revelers in anachronism.
They don't want you here. They

want to be left alone with egrets,
　　　heron, the great salt marsh.
But oh, down the road, great #1,
　　　twists and hums, OM, like
the Beatniks of your dreams,

California dreaming, yes,
shadows of Cathedral Grove,
        the dark Bohemian trees,
epiphany of Redwoods, surrounds
        you, and you are on fire,
from your toe-nails to hair follicles.
        Redwood rhapsody. Listen—
the Sleeping Maiden sings your name.

Again, On The Road To Tillamook

Heading west from Portland
to Tillamook, a Zen rain on the windshield,
the wipers syncopating
like the radio's jazz, the thick
musky air infiltrating
the Skylark's gray chambers.
Dave Brubeck's West Coast Cool rains,
your fingers tapping the steering wheel,
and suddenly I'm whistling
a riff, rolling down the windows,
catching a cool spray against my shoulder,
thinking of a question
to steer us through the mountains,
deciding on no talk. Just jazz
and soybean fields rolling by,
the blue mountains' rim of sun,
a slash of amber cloud and hint of moon.
Then we're really in the thick of it,
burning pipe, the riff of water over rock.
Then Sonny Rollins and the silence of elk;
and we're blinking past Lee's Camp Store,
where the radio waves give up the ghost.
All stillness and the Pacific's tug.
We have mastered this: driving
Highway 26 toward the sea, driving
where the even the jazz can't follow us
to the other side, a pasture of cows,
skunk cabbage, the rich odor of Tillamook.
Just ahead, where we can go
no further, the sea, the sea.

At Home After A Journey West

In jet-lag consciousness
that sweet inertia
not unlike morphine, and if
I get lucky
and don't have to work the next day,
then comes the delicious bonus
of a homecoming to savor:
vanilla coffee in the wheel thrown mug
from the potter in Ellison Bay,
the open garret window
where an April bluster billows
the blue gauze curtains,
all the old, refinished oak—
the big desk where I write longhand,
the curved hutch filled with magic,
a traveler's treasure trove of antique crystal,
swan and golden-laced Nippons.
                              Then the drift
back to Sausalito, its purple princess flowers,
the bay, and San Francisco across it.
A bakery's mixed blessings in breezes,
and now toast browning here at home,
where a cat named Maybe sabotages the phone
near the big bed with its firm mattress.
In that jet-lag afterglow, I
light a wand of sandalwood incense,
exfoliate with eucalyptus shower gel,
slip into clean white underwear.
We travelers juggle our prodigal joys:
what was new grew wingspan,
what we return to a nest
of history and good fortune—
sweetest red ruby grapefruit,
the good sharp knife,
the burst of citrus.

Lighthouse

When Midwest air threatens strangling,
and green breath of plants suffocate,
when black, practical earth no longer satisfies,
despite relentless fertility,
and the garden seems more weed than yield,
when I cannot tell where drone of locust
and chain saw end and inner ear begins,
when muddy rivers aren't enough,
and black specks of sweat roll into
little cigars on my neck,
I go in search of lighthouses;
there is a lighthouse muse within:
a keeper of the water,
the eye of lake, bay, or ocean,
a tall steel cow bellowing.
She is guardian of sand dunes,
counter of tides,
conscience of fisherman and sailors,
mourner of sunken hulls
whose bones harbor murky playgrounds.
I go to see her,
to walk theses shores,
until wind burned, I empty
my humidity into air
and freeze my feet to numbness
in lapping tongues of clear water.
Then my skin fits again.
I return to dig potatoes
in black, tumid earth,
to pick tomato medallions
on this garden prayer rug
pointed to that lighthouse.

Among the Trees With Charity

Summer Solstice

A pair of Green Comma Angel Wing butterflies cavorting
around the pear tree, the young pears aureola-rosy.
Everywhere another shade of green pipes a Celtic jig.
A patch of catnip lures a tawny Angora cat
with a gorgeous black mask. I love to see him
rolling in the driveway, chasing the crows
who have eaten all the spring-pink, bristly strawberries.
Raccoons resume night marauding, lead their kin
to the skylight to sleep, peep down on us.
Now the air's obese with birdsong and an embarrassment
of old peonies, day-sleeping fireflies cradled on leaves.
I sleep in too, listen to obscure female singers
whose names escape me. Plans slip away, disappear
like barrel slugs. Each sunset brings angel wings.
Mars travels closer to the earth in the southeast horizon,
blinks by Antares, now orange as a field lily.
A Question Mark Angel Wing butterfly spends time
cozied on my arm. Everywhere the undersides of leaves
quietly tending larvae. Listen. Nighthawks whistle.
The squirrels are changing from red to gray. Listen.
The Earth says Yes and No and Yes again.
It's a month of Sundays but I skip church,
drive Wisconsin country roads alone,
catch an old Janis Joplin tune, and maybe cry.
She's singing Try just a little bit harder now,
but I can't force the bulb of my life to open
any further into a season altogether out of my control.

What A Gardener Knows About Change

Sometimes an urge burns to rip
        the whole damn mess out. Tear
trumpet vine from the cozy cove it's taken over.
           Snare snaggled junipers from crooked roots.

Put the overgrown flowering quince
        out of its misery. Poison
every prolific ivy: yellow archangel,
          grape, English ivy, Virginia creeper.

Let the squirrels eat each tulip
        & bury each lily bulb. Throw out
mossy wooden tubs that hold water hyacinth.
        Simply burn the ferns.

Recant all unruly roses.
        Remove the hens & chicks
from their nests around driveway rocks.
        Ferret out the peonies and phlox.

Divorce the bridal wreath bush.
        Chop down the yellow maple, the old pear,
the river birch and imperfect pines.
        But then the gardener recalls all the time

& all the care the whole beautiful mess took:
        how the trumpet vine wound four years
before its orange song blared from the archway,
        two more to lure a hummingbird.

How juniper berries frost in autumn
        & wink green eyes in January. How only
the lucky ever grow a flowering quince
        & someday surely there will be time to make

fragrant quince jelly. Or the gardener might
            reconcile: without ivy, bricks would be bricks,
cement would be cement & no ivy-laced
            bungalow would entreat a poet's dreams.

Squirrels bury bulbs where they choose anyway.
            Last year a Queen of Night graced the alley.
Lo, lilies of the field quell worry
            in their tight buds & all summer

old neighbors watch for water hyacinth
            & fern fronds stretch feathers of shade.
Hens & chicks remind us that there's scrappy
            beauty in the commonplace & a garden

without phlox has fewer monarchs & no chance
            to catch a morning striped sphinx moth.
Each June the bridal wreath bush explodes like popcorn.
            The Midwest is a barren place without trees,

so the gardener makes many small decisions:
            a thinning here, a transplant there,
extras to friends or compost. We pull weeds,
            scatter mulch and know that change

is the tailspin of tiny transformations,
            the endless blessing of rearrangement.

After The Tornado Sky

Wind sheer,
ferocious lighting cracking trunks of old maples,
slashing branches from honey locust trees,
ripping large pines right from their roots,
freezing clocks at 4:25 a.m.
Dawn after the Tornado Sky.
First the birds cried tentatively.
For a long while squirrels didn't show their faces.
I feared they might have perished,
nests toppling with 100-mile an hour winds
that roared through the city like bombers.
All morning the birdcalls grew stronger.
I imagined they cried, "Where are you?
I'm over here. Here. Here."
The scrappy crows were loudest and tenacious,
their feathers iridescent as they poked
through soggy grass. The sparrows too
found their way back to the feeders.
A red hawk refugee
from Sinnissippi Park, where pummeled tress lay
like soldiers on a battlefield, landed on a shepherd's hook.
Where was the ruby-throated hummingbird
who had befriended me?
My sweet, little garden companion, feeding
at her favorite scarlet bergamot throughout the day.
I wondered how her nest, the size of a penny,
woven from cobwebs, and the twin eggs
as tiny as ticktack mints, met the storm.
I wondered where all the nesting creatures went,
and my heart filled like a storm cloud
needing to burst.
The hummingbird returned, early evening.
She saw me at the window, rose up,

a micro-helicopter near my face.
I like to think she said,
"I'm here. We made it."
Though I haven't seen the flicker,
the chickadees and purple finches are landing
on the tilted lilacs and ragged yellow pine.
Sometimes a streak of yellow signals
a goldfinch by the tender sunflower shoots.
A catbird meows somewhere in a thicket
of conifers. The squirrels walk on telephone wires
like trapeze artists without balancing poles.

Let Indian Summer Come

For Jane Kenyon

Let Indian Summer blaze through brown grass blades.
Let it ripple around all that is gold:
field corn drying on stalks,
all the russet maiden grass on plains,
the amber seed heads of goldenrod and aster.
Let Indian Summer come.

Let it come burning the sun's last hot rays
to the red pony's black muddy hooves,
to the pink snouts of possums asleep behind logs,
to fuzzy fountain grasses swaying in prairies.
Let it slant down on blue spruce and white pine.
Let Indian Summer come.

Let it come whispering on tabby cat whiskers,
tippling moss-coated trunks of maples,
shimmering on small red crab apples in meadows,
landing and looping with groups of cedar waxwings
on their trek from Wisconsin to the Carolinas.
Let Indian Summer come.

Let it arc over Rock River bluffs and castle rocks,
over every circling bird of prey.
Let it glint from the eagle's chartreuse eye
and glimmer from the red hawk's splayed tail.
Let it soar wide as the vulture's black wingspan.
Let Indian Summer come.

Let it come in full head-dress, thundering.
Let it drum full color on leaves
rattle and shake fall's last tassels.
Let it shout. Let it whoop and whirl.
All creatures deserve one final dance in the sun.
So let Indian Summer come.

Amidst Prairie Grass

Soft mounds of maiden grass give way
to lacey tassels, swaying
and sashaying
in October's wily wind
near the black-eyed susans spiraling
inward in dark, dry stalks.
Seed heads like caterpillars burst
from fountain grass, and on the last purple
of the butterfly bush, a monarch—
sun on black-veined wings.
Muhlenbergia filipes.
Pennesetum setaceum Rubrum.
Micanthus sinensis Gracillimus.
Even the names of prairie grass
are benedictions in the Midwest,
where sometimes the azure sky
wraps around us like a dome,
so close we're in the thick of it,
why we love fall the best
with its drama of transformation,
the prairie grass with its wide salutation
to the sun, Indian Summer hoofing
through golden spears and reeds,
rippling the Ravenna grass,
pounding the pampas grass.
Oceans of grasses singing like gypsies.
Frosted grasses glistening,
rooted in the pungent, black earth.
Deep within a great labyrinth unseen,
so much goes on without us—
a blade of prairie grass,
a shaft of wheat,
river ways of roots and tubes,

mondo grass returning to its source,
seed heads bursting,
a single seed sleeping until next year.
And I say again today amidst prairie grass:
So much goes on without us.

October Morning

The street is quiet as cotton here,
Today, and the air Nordic sweet—
A luscious alchemy of blue spruce,
White pine, Russian sage, lemon mint
And lavender gone to seed, blended
With smoky leaves and woods of autumn.
Here the prairie garden wraps around us
With its limber maiden grasses, its tassels
Like a hundred wish-granting wands.
Hardy mauve sedum and goldenrod.
Let morning meander through lacey
Honey locusts as water trickles beneath
The periwinkle myrtle that winds
Beneath the serviceberry tree. Let
One red-veined leaf float
From the sunset maple and land
On the birdbath's lip. Let its yellow
Complications land like cabbage moths.
Let this day begin.

Winter Spell

When Venus glides by Mars, and seven planets
          stitch a diamond necklace
under Capricorn in the southwest twilight,
          and a tangerine moon rises
like a Phoenix through murky clouds, find

a Depression Glass vase. Imagine the Italian
          mid-wife who kept it near her canary
long before you were born. Listen to them.
          Recite all the blessings of the year,
even those you didn't wish for. Especially those.

Place bittersweet and Chinese lanterns
          in the vase, invoking lost loves
that have brought you to this cold enchantment.
          Lay the vase on a window sill where
the moon casts long shadows through the trees,

and a cat with one good eye might sleep
          curled in a grapevine basket
next to THE DREAMER'S DICTIONARY.
          Find the last five dreams you can
remember, reading their meanings softly.

Arrange them into a story that begins with
          "Once upon a time in the land of"
and ends with "lived happily ever after."
          Tell the story to someone you long for.
Then, looking out the window, remember

footprints in hard-packed snow: cat, deer,
    rabbit, raccoon, crow, sparrow.
Remember them as you brew hot tea—
    mint, chamomile, and rosehips—
in a Nippon teapot from Goodwill.

As the tea steeps, find a ring of moonstone,
    opal or coral and a red woolen scarf.
Wearing them, mix a potent of pepper, nut-
    meg and curry in a wooden bowl.
Sprinkle the doorway and sneeze thrice.

Sing a song from childhood. Any song
    will do. Return to the tea, adding
milk and honey before you drink it slowly.
    When steam fogs the window, no
evil shall enter where only the enchanted live.

A Christmas Reflection

I walk down the cold basement stairs,
'tis the season to be jolly on my mind.
When I open the cool closet doors,
familiar musty shelves of boxes,
crates of memories and junk sift together
like the butter cookies I no longer eat.

Scrawled on the crumbling cardboard—
Textbooks, Jamaica, Wedding, Will,
Christmas, Christmas, Christmas,
Dusty, plastic holly cascades from one.
A too cute Santa winks from another,
his good eye stolen by the cat.

Twenty years of grab bags, office parties.
So many well-intentioned little gifts.
So bless the craftomaniacs who slide
into my life like Jehovah Witnesses,
who leave these messages I'm still too nice
to throw away. Yes, bless them.

But not this year. No. Today I'll choose
Just one—a small, crystal manger scene
And close the chilly doors with a snap
Scurry up the stairs. I'll place it
On white lace of the old dining room table
Nestled among the four Advent candles.

When I turn on the Tiffany rose chandelier,
Prisms sparkle. Stars on the ceiling!
Lo! How a rose e'er blooming!
I light candles in the warm room
This year, softly humming *Tis a gift*
To be simple. Tis a gift to be free . . .

January Rain, 2002

Zen rain on cedar shingles.
January in the Midwest.
Winter has not yet come
with its down comforter of snow,
its peace like a pleasant dream
piped on a clear, cold night
after love under Antares.
Rain scratching its talons
on the skylight, where an ash
small as a cabbage moth lands.
No one, not even the cat
craning to see it from above,
knows what this renegade filigree
can be, blown in from the northeast.
Perhaps the heart of a computer wizard
cremated in the stairwell last September
on the fiftieth floor? Is this too
morbid? Then let's talk
of the gibbous moon last November,
how it drooped like a storm cloud,
the way you feel when the blues
blows its bitter wind against your temple.
It's raining in January.
A wise man returns from his morning walk
with rain on his boots
and a mouth like a waning moon.
Seeing his frown, his wife asks what's wrong.
Global warning he says. If
you look deeply, you will see
Illinois turning into Mississippi.
That's how the blues hits
this January when it's raining,
here in the kitchen
where you slice an apple in half
to find a perfect starburst of seeds.

One Cold February Morning

Venus, the morning star, brilliant
in the indigo east horizon.
Winter dawn in the Midwest.
Through bare, black trees, crimson
flashes like the rings of Saturn.
The sun rises, a dome over
the huge blue spruce that has stood
like a monolith for half a century
in the neighbor's back yard.
Jack the Dog, a young white shepherd,
sniffs the crab apple's motley trunk,
urinates with gusto. A clumsy gold
calligraphy on snow.
It's 15 degrees. A small bird sings, nestled
deep within the white pine's ice-glistening
branches. Over the wires that separate
backyards in this quiet neighborhood,
a helicopter with its precious cargo
and terrible turbulence head its way
to the hospital landing. Heroic people
will pull a person, not yet called The Body,
out on a stretcher. A crow lands on black
cable wire. Smoke, like dancing ghosts,
bellows from our collective chimneys.

Where This Early Spring Morning Took
An Unsuspecting Poem

Early this March morning, the cardinal red against
Dried stalks of pampas grass that sway
In the benevolent wind, ripe with conglomerate birdsong
And O, such promise.
                              Though it's best to cut
The grassy peacocks down to their nubby green spears,
What romantic gardener can bear the thought:
Those glorious tassels chopped, no more dancing harems
In the garden. We sit ambivalent, longing always
For the moment's last sustained grace.
                              What luxury, what desirable life,
To have time to thirst for beauty
Like hummingbirds thirst for red nectar. Of course
The nectar's not really red. It's the illusion
Of attraction. Red, like love early
In its course.
                              What luck, what desirable life, when red
Gives way to sustenance, sweet nectar drawing us back
Time and again.
                              I remember a hummingbird that flew
Right to my lips, painted "Red, Frosted Berries" that day.
Another torpedoed to my scraped knee,
First to discover its red mushroom of blood. I am in love
With the hummingbird and can't bring this poem back
To the pampas grass, can't muster specific wisdom,
And this poem is like pampas grass, swaying,
Still long enough to hold a few birds
In this desirable life.

This April Morning

"It seems possible to live
simply on this earth."
— Charles Simic

I love to wake without alarm,
Open the window by the bed,
Find April arriving, the garden
Thriving with crocus and cardinal.

Now a speckled dove traverses
Nubby, sheered prairie grass.
Sparrows nest in blue spruce.
Inside, wind rustling white curtains.

Outside, children with backpacks
Trundling off to school, where
At least one teacher will show kindness
To that little soldier who finds

This thick spring day, well,
Just a bit too much. The tiniest
Black and white bees burrow
Little volcanoes around tree roots.

Good neighbor Tom says they're harmless,
Good for the garden he tells me.
Why, they eat pests beneath dark soil—
Ones you didn't even know were there.

You have known places dark
As Illinois soil, where the ice over-stayed
Its welcome. Who hasn't who walks
Among the trees with charity?

You too have lived largely
Like the old magnolia, its pink-saucer
Fragrance of paradise.
The good bees buzzing.

About the Author

Christine Swanberg has published several books of poetry: *Tonight On This Late Road* (Erie St., 1984), *Invisible String* (Erie St., 1990), *Bread Upon The Waters* (UW: Whitewater, 1990), *Slow Miracle* (Lake Shore, 1992), *The Tenderness Of Memory* (Plainview Press, 1995), *The Red Lacquer Room* (Chiron Press, 2001.) Her work appears in anthologies such as *Knowing Stones: Poems of Exotic Travel, I Am Becoming The Woman I've Wanted, Jane's Stories, Key West: An Anthology*, and *Pride and Joy*. Over 250 poems have been published in 70 journals such as *The Beloit Poetry Journal, Spoon River Quarterly, Amelia, Chiron*, and others. Awards include *Poetswest, Peninsula Pulse, Midwest Poetry Review, Nit and Wit*, and the Connor Award for Fiction as well as a Merit Scholarship in Poetry from Vermont College. She has edited *Korone, Confluence: A Legacy of Rock River Valley; Land: Connections*, and Rock River Poetry Contest.

She has been a teacher for over thirty years and has mentored many young and adult writers. Along with poetry, her passions include singing, gardening, swimming, and traveling. With her husband, Jeffrey, she has traveled widely to many continents. For many years, she was an avid equestrian. She currently lives a quiet, simple life with Jeffrey, her husband of 33 years, in Rockford, Illinois.

CPSIA information can be obtained at www.ICGtesting.com
Printed in the USA
238720LV00003B/7/A